Young Talents of Uzbekistan

Tukhtaev Sardor

© Tukhtaev Sardor
Young Talents of Uzbekistan
by: Tukhtaev Sardor
Edition: June '2024
Publisher:
Taemeer Publications LLC (Michigan, USA / Hyderabad, India)

ISBN 978-93-5872-258-1

© **Tukhtaev Sardor**

Book	:	Young Talents of Uzbekistan
Author	:	Tukhtaev Sardor
Publisher	:	Taemeer Publications
Year	:	'2024
Pages	:	70
Title Design	:	*Taemeer Web Design*

Table of contents

1. Nimatillayev Mohichehra………………………………………

2. Intizor Inattulayeva……………………………………………

3. Shodiyev Sevinch………………………………………………

4. Alisherova Dilshoda……………………………………………

5. Shodiyeva Madina………………………………………………

6. Jumaboyeva Navruza……………………………………………

7. Hatamova Charos Shavkatjon qizi……………………………

8. Avazbekova Mubinabonu Dilshodbek qizi……………………

9. Sobirjonova Sevinch Akmaljon qizi……………………………

10. Yusufjonov Bahrom……………………………………………

Nimatillayeva Mohichehra Zafarjan Qizi is a first-year student in the Faculty of Chinese Studies at the Tashkent State University of Oriental Studies. Born on October 30, 2005, in the city of Navoi. He can speak Russian, English, Uzbek, and Tajik fluently. He is currently studying Chinese. He participated in the 2021 Youth Forum of Uzbekistan as a youth ambassador. In his youth, several poems and stories were published in local newspapers and magazines. Her score on IELTS is 6.5.

Enduring Partnership: Uzbekistan and China on the Silk Road and Beyond

Annotation: This article will cover cooperation between Uzbekistan and China and the universal values and ties of the Commonwealth of countries.

Keywords: "Great Silk Road", national values, Chinese language

Commonwealth relations in the Asian countries of Uzbekistan and China go back to ancient times. In particular, the relations between China and the country of Davan (Fergana), which began in the 5th and 4th centuries, later played an important role in the emergence of the "Great Silk Road," which connects the countries of the East and West. This route, which for 1,500 years connected countries not only through trade but also through science and a number of discoveries, later led to a further strengthening of diplomatic relations with the "Min" dynasty in China, even under the Great Prince Amir Temur. In 2023-2027, relations aimed at the development of strategic freedom between Uzbekistan and China, as part of the educational system, culture, tourism, and trade, are equally opening up wide opportunities for both peoples. Hardworking, devoted, selfless, and humane, the Chinese and Uzbek people have similarities in historical, political, educational, everyday life, and family values. The familiarity of the Chinese people, respect for the elderly, the fact that young people will definitely seek advice from older people in the family before making an important decision, and the high position of the elderly in each family as a separate family are in harmony with our Uzbek values. After all, we can also respect the elderly in Uzbekistan and give young people Just as each Eastern country honors its national history and past centuries later, China values its centuries-old empires and its sages, who have not yet lost their influence in the daily life- and politics of China. In particular, the main principle of the organization of Chinese society, an integral part of the way of life, the recognition of the wise Confucius, who is still considered the basis of Chinese civilization, as a "great teacher," also proves how literally the Uzbek people memorize such great ancestors as the Noble Emir Temur and Alisher Navoi. In order for the younger generation in China not to forget the ancient traditions, Confucian institutions, media shows on Confucian life, the application of Confucian textbooks in schools and universities, the establishment of the Timurians School of 2019 with the decisions of the president of our country, and proof of the uniqueness of the goal envisaged by such decisions as establishing the subjects of etiquette in the educational system, Our great-great-grandfather Alisher is inextricably linked with the wise words of Nawai: "Man cannot live in life forever, but can leave a good name after himself," the instructive word of the Chinese folk sage Confucius in the sense of "striving for humanity, repelling man from all the evils of this world." In addition, in his speech, the Chinese people's Chairman, Xi Jinping, singled out Chinese folk proverbs, even noting the similarity between Uzbek folk proverbs. For example, 关键看老乡 "it depends on ordinary people whether there will be prosperity or not." There are similar types of proverbs in Uzbek, such as "power is in unity," "united self, uniting dust," and if brothers act together, they can even come in gold. These proverbs are aimed at calling the people to solidarity. There is a proverb among the Uzbek people: "Only trees filled with fruits attract attention." Through this proverb, the comprehensive cooperation between China and Uzbekistan has already paid off, noting that there is a way to lead the two peoples to happiness, as well as the fact that the trust and support of the population of the two states have been achieved by the chairman of the PRC in his speech. The great allomas that have matured in Uzbekistan, notably Muhammad Babur, Jaloliddin Manguberdi, and Abu Ali Ibn- Sino, are very well known and respected in China. A vivid manifestation of our national literature, on the occasion of the 130th anniversary of the birth of the founder of Uzbek national romanticism, Abdullah Qadiri, Adib's novels "past days" and "Scorpio from Love" are recognized for their translation into Chinese.Translated works in collaboration, published in large circulation by the publishing house of the Social Sciences of the People's Republic of China. Due to the increased interest of young people in the study of Chinese in Uzbekistan, the education system provides a strong basis for the inter-state ava teacher exchange programs, the establishment of Confucian institutions in Tashkent and Samarkand for the effective learning of Chinese by young people, the training of sixronic translators between China and Uzbekistan, and friendship between both countries.

Literature used:

1. Jeremy Page's 2015 Wall Street Journal, "Why is China turning back to Confucius?"
2. https://archive.uz/post/xitoy-ozbekiston-dostligining-yangi-yorqin-sahifalari
3. Article: "Bringing Traditional Chinese to Life"
4. Tom 3 No. 1 Part 1 (2023): Eurasian Journal of Social Sciences, Philosophy, and Culture
5. Central Asia and ancient China relations: the emergence of the Great Silk Road | Eurasiysky Journal Sosialnix Nauk, filosofii I kulturi 6. 7. https://in-academy.uz/index.php/ejsspc/article/view/8365

Intizor Inatullayeva is an 11th-grade student of specialized boarding school №1 of Navoi city

If you want to take the sky,
Why don't you hold my shoulder.

Sh.M.Mirziyoyev

Currently, the number of schools in our Republic is about 11 000. The number of specialized schools in the public education system has reached 790. In addition, 14 Presidential schools operate in our country. With the initiatives of our honorable president, in order to introduce the environment and methodology of Presidential schools to other schools are gradually being transferred to the system of the Presidential education agency. Today, the number of such schools in our country has reached 182.

It is no exaggeration to say that thanks to this reform, which was carried out by the initative of our President, many opportunities have been opened for students. Among them, I am a graduate of specialized boarding school №1 of Navoi city. The classrooms of our school are spacious bright and equipped with the necessary information and communication tools. Students are provided with free accommodation and food is free for all students. Thanks to the educational system, the skills of pedagogues, and the behavior of students, the students of our schools are have been achieving many awards. In the 2022-2023 academic year, 14 students of the boarding school took pride of place at the regional stage of the Science Olympiad. 4 students of the boarding school took part in the second qualifying round of the International Olympiad, 2 of them won the ticket to the next round. In this academic year, 5 students of our school won prizes at the Olympiad of PDP University. In the 2023-2024 academic year, 4 students won the first place, 2 students won the second place, and 4 students won the third place at the regional stage of the Science Olympiad. Boarding school students won silver and bronze medals at SEAMO International Asian Olympiad. Currently, 36 students of the boarding school have international and national certificates of English proficiency, 16 students have SAT certificates.

The difference between specialized schools and other schools is that students and pedagogues are accepted on the basis of tests and certain subjects are taught in depth. As the President of the Republic of Uzbekistan, Shavkat Miromonovich Mirziyoyev, said " Education will not develop as long as we do not put it on its feet". We young people will build the future of new Uzbekistan, the foundations of the third Reneissance. It is our duty to fulfill the President's trust and to make unceasing efforts to become a well qualified person for the country by utilizing all of the opportunities wisely.

My full name is Shodiyeva Sevinch Pahlavon qizi. I was born in Tashkent and currently live in Kitab, Kashkadarya region. I am sixteen years old. I am a student of the eleventh grade. 07.06.2007. Student.

Sometimes even things without a soul cry.

This rain, which is covered with black clouds and raining in buckets, probably does not leave vivid memories for everyone. Because of the rain, someone's work was delayed, someone's plans were ruined, and someone else's life was filled with rain.It can be said that these rains are a strange decoration of autumn, a charming shine. It brings a special feeling to every heart.It's funny, for some reason, when it rains. Many people say that the sky is crying. Isn't it just a natural phenomenon? Can they cry? If that is the case, that is, if things in nature cry, then they also have a soul. Maybe even the sun that shines from early morning cries every day. We think that the leaves of the trees fall when autumn comes. We know that people shed tears, maybe trees shed their leaves instead of tears. Maybe they miss spring and cry.

Want to bite? We say that men cannot cry. Maybe the lightnings, like them, are filling the world with noise, unable to cope with these pains that make their stomach tremble. That tiny red flower? Although the liver was full of red blood, it was open with laughter. Maybe he's crying when he wakes up. You may find it hard to digest some books, some pages may be unfamiliar to you. Maybe every line of this book is crying.

Because the writer's pages are running out, the life of the pen is running out, because winter can't warm his hands, spring can't wear boots and play in the snow, because some seas don't have ships (some ships don't have seas), some bodies don't have bodies, souls , the horizon is crying because it misses someone.

Maybe the night has turned into darkness because it misses the day...

Alisherova Dilshoda Azizxon qizi was born in 2003 in Namangan region of Uzbekistan. Dilshoda was a pupil of Ibrat school which specialized foreign languages. She is a participant, advisor, delegate, coordinator, volunteer-translator. She is a member of "IYES Foundation" "IQRA" "Juntos por Las Letras" "Asih Sasami Indonesia Global Writers". She has own projects with names "Liderliksirlari1 - Secret of
leadership" Top_scholar". She had experience in American Corner Namangan with topic "Leaders of ACN" as trainer. She took nomination of "The

Best Coordinator" of Ibrat camp and she is a taker of a badge with name " Initiative reformer" from UN. Besides that, she is a silver medal winner of SEAMO(South East Asian Math Olimpiad). Dilshoda is a stipendium of "Student of the Year2022"

Uzbekistan state world languages university
English language №3 faculty
Theoretical aspects of English language №3 department

FINAL ON Foreign literature

Theme: Alex's Journey
Group: 2146

Full name: Alisherova DilshodaAs the first in his family to attend college, Alex was determined to make the most of this opportunity. He was filled with a mixture of excitement and anxiety as he prepared to leave for the prestigious Northwood University, known for its rigorous programs and vibrant campus life.From a young age, Alex had shown a keen interest in science and technology. His room was a testament to his passions, with shelves lined with science fiction novels and a desk cluttered with homemade gadgets. His parents, though supportive, had little understanding of his ambitions. His father worked long hours as a mechanic, and his mother juggled multiple jobs to keep the family afloat. They were proud of Alex's achievements, yet apprehensive about the unknown world he was about to enter.The night before his departure, Alex couldn't sleep. He lay in bed, staring at the ceiling, his mind racing with thoughts of what lay ahead.Would he fit in? Would he be able to handle the academic pressure? More importantly, would he find a place where he truly belonged? Despite his doubts, he knew one thing for certain: this was his chance to turn his dreams into reality.The day Alex arrived at Northwood University was a bright, sunny day. The campus was bustling with activity as new students moved into their dorms, parents offering last-minute advice and farewells. Alex's dormitory,

Hawthorne Hall, was a historic building with ivy-covered walls and a large common area where students gathered. He felt a mix of nervousness and excitement as he walked through the hallways, finding his room on the third floor.

His roommate, Mark, was already there, unpacking his belongings. Mark was a tall, athletic guy with a friendly smile. They quickly hit it off, sharing stories about their hometowns and aspirations.Mark was from a big city and seemed confident and outgoing, a stark contrast to Alex's more reserved nature. Despite their differences, they found common ground in their love for basketball and video games.After settling in, Alex decided to explore the campus. The university was even more impressive than he had imagined. The sprawling lawns, state-of-the-art facilities, and the historic library filled him with a sense of awe. As he wandered around, he couldn't help but feel a sense of pride and anticipation. This was the place where he would build his future, where he would find out what he was truly capable of.The orientation week was a whirlwind of activities designed to help new students acclimate to university life. Alex attended various workshops and social events, making new friends and learning about the resources available to him.

The academic advising session was particularly insightful, as he got to meet some of his professors and learn about the courses he would be taking. By the end of the week, Alex felt more confident and ready to embark on his college journey.The initial excitement of being at Northwood University soon gave way to the harsh realities of academic life. Alex found himself struggling with the rigorous coursework and the fast-paced nature of his classes. Despite his passion for science and technology, the sheer volume of assignments and the level of detail required was overwhelming. He spent countless hours in the library, often late into the night, trying to keep up with his studies.Socially, things were also challenging. While he had made a few friends during orientation week, he found it difficult to connect with people on a deeper level. Most of his classmates seemed confident and self-assured, while Alex often felt like he was pretending to fit in.The initial homesickness he experienced didn't help either. He missed his family and the familiar comforts of home. Phone calls with his parents provided some solace, but they also reminded him of the distance between them.One evening, after a particularly tough day, Alex sat alone in his dorm room, feeling defeated. He had just received a poor grade on his first major assignment, and it felt like a confirmation of his worst fears. Maybe he wasn't cut out for this. Maybe he had been wrong to dream so big. As these thoughts swirled in his mind, there was a knock on the door. It was Mark, who had noticed

Alex's struggles and offered a listening ear. They talked for hours, and for the first time, Alex felt a glimmer of hope. Maybe he wasn't alone in this after all.The turning point for Alex came when he attended a guest lecture by Dr. Eleanor Hayes, a renowned professor in the Computer Science department. Dr. Hayes was not only an expert in her field but also known for her ability to inspire and mentor students. Her lecture on artificial intelligence was captivating, and Alex found himself hanging on to every word. After the lecture, he gathered the courage to approach her and express his admiration for her work.Dr. Hayes was approachable and encouraging. She listened to Alex's concerns and offered him valuable advice. She suggested that he join her research group, which focused on cutting-edge AI technologies. Alex was thrilled at the opportunity and eagerly accepted. This marked the beginning of a transformative period in his college journey. Under Dr. Hayes' mentorship, he began to see his studies in a new light.She taught him how to approach problems methodically and encouraged him to think critically and creatively.Being part of the research group also allowed Alex to connect with other students who shared his interests. He found a supportive community where he could share ideas and collaborate on projects. The group meetings were intellectually stimulating and provided a sense of belonging that Alex had been yearning for. Slowly but surely, he started to regain his confidence.Just as things were starting to look up for Alex, he faced a major setback. During a critical phase of a research project, his laptop crashed, resulting in the loss of several weeks' worth of data. Despite having backups, some of the most recent work was irretrievable. The incident left Alex devastated and questioning his ability to succeed in such a demanding field.Dr. Hayes, however, was a source of unwavering support. She reminded him that setbacks are an integral part of any learning process. Together, they formulated a plan to recover as much data as possible and to prevent such incidents in the future. Alex also received help from his peers, who pitched in with their own notes and resources. This experience, though painful, taught him valuable lessons about resilience and the importance of community.During this period, Alex also leaned heavily on the friendships he had formed. Mark, in particular, proved to be a steadfast friend, encouraging Alex to take breaks and reminding him of his progress. Despite the setback, Alex felt a renewed sense of determination. He realized that his journey was about more than just academic success; it was about learning to navigate challenges and growing stronger in the process.Determined to turn things around, Alex adopted a more disciplined approach to his studies and personal life. He developed a study schedule that balanced his coursework, research, and downtime.Dr. Hayes introduced him to mindfulness practices that helped reduce stress and improve focus. Alex also started attending workshops on time management and productivity offered by the university's student support services.One of the most significant changes was his decision to join a campus club focused on innovation and entrepreneurship. The club members were a diverse group of students from various disciplines, all passionate about turning ideas into reality.Working on collaborative projects reignited Alex's creativity and provided a practical outlet for his skills. He began to see how the theoretical knowledge he was gaining could be applied to solve real-world problems.As Alex's confidence grew, so did his willingness to take on new challenges. He volunteered to lead a team project in one of his courses, which involved designing a prototype for a sustainable energy solution. This project required extensive research, teamwork, and presentation skills. Under his leadership, the team worked tirelessly, and their project was eventually selected for a university-wide innovation showcase.

With each passing semester, Alex's grades improved, and so did his overall outlook on college life. The balance he had struck between academics, research, and extracurricular activities proved to be effective.His involvement in the innovation club led to several successful projects, earning him recognition among his peers and professors.Alex also became more socially active, attending campus events and building stronger friendships. The support system he developed played a crucial role in his personal growth.

He realized that asking for help was not a sign of weakness but a strength. His relationship with Mark deepened, and they often reflected on their journeys and future aspirations.The most rewarding experience came when Alex was invited to present his research at a national conference. It was an opportunity to showcase his work to a broader audiene confidence he needed. The presentation was a success, and Alex received positive feedback and valuable insights from attendees.Just as Alex began to feel comfortable in his new rhythm, another significant challenge arose. The university announced a major hackathon, inviting students to develop innovative solutions to global problems within 48 hours.Thecompetition was fierce, with teams from various universities participating. Alex saw this as an opportunity to test his skills and push his boundaries.Forming a team with members from the innovation club, Alex took on the role of team leader. The problem they chose to address was related to water scarcity, aiming to develop a smart system for water conservation in urban areas.

The intense 48-hour period tested their technical skills, creativity, and ability to work under pressure.Despite meticulous planning, they encountered numerous technical glitches andunexpected hurdles. The team was exhausted and frustrated, and at one point, it seemed like they might not complete the project.Alex, drawing on the resilience he had built over the past semesters, kept the team motivated. He reminded them of their collective strength and their ability to overcome obstacles.

In the final hours of the hackathon, Alex's team managed to pull everything together. Their prototype worked, and they were able to present a functional demo to the judges. The judges were impressed by the ingenuity and practicality of their solution.

When the results were announced, Alex's team won first place, earning not only a monetary prize but also recognition and offers for internships from several companies.

heThis victory was a turning point for Alex. It was a testament to his growth and the skills had developed. The experience of leading a team and successfully navigating a high-pressure environment gave him newfound confidence. It also opened doors to new opportunities, including Alex's success was celebrated by his friends, mentors, and family. His parents, who had always been supportive but unsure of his path, were immensely proud. They saw the transformation in their son and realized that his dreams were not only achievable but were becoming a reality. As Alex approached the end of his college journey, he took time to reflect on his experiences. The challenges he faced and the successes he achieved had shaped him in ways he never imagined. He realized that the true value of his education lay not just in the knowledge he gained, but in the resilience, adaptability, and confidence he developed. Alex decided to pursue a career in sustainable technology, driven by the passion he discovered during his time at Northwood University. He set new goals for himself, including furthering his education with a graduate degree and working on projects that could make a tangible impact on the world.

His journey had taught him the importance of perseverance, community, and the continuous pursuit of knowledge. Graduation day was a moment of pride and joy. As he walked across the stage to receive his diploma, he thought about the path that had brought him here. The friendships, the mentorship, the setbacks, and the triumphs were all part of a journey that was uniquely his own. Alex knew that the road ahead would have its own challenges, but he was ready to face them with the same determination and optimism that had brought him this far. After the hackathon victory, Alex's life at Northwood University continued to flourish. He was now recognized as a leader in the innovation community on campus, and this opened up many new opportunities.One such opportunity was an invitation to participate in an international student exchange program. Alex eagerly accepted the chance to spend a semester at the prestigious Technische Universität in Munich, Germany.The experience abroad was both exhilarating and challenging. Alex had to adapt to a new culture, language, and academic environment. The exposure to different perspectives and cutting-edge technologies broadened his understanding of sustainable solutions.He collaborated with students and professors from around the world, sharing knowledge and gaining insights that would be invaluable for his futojects . Living in a foreign country also pushed Alex out of his comfort zone, fostering personal growth. He made new friends, explored historic cities, and even learned some German. The experience taught him the importance of adaptability and open-mindedness, traits that would serve him well in his future career.Returning to Northwood for his final year, Alex felt a renewed sense of purpose. He was determined to make the most of his remaining time and decided to focus his efforts on a capstone project that combined his passion for technology and sustainability.He proposed a project to develop a smart grid system for managing renewable energy sources, which garnered enthusiastic support from Dr. Hayes and the department.Alex assembled a team of like-minded students and began working on the project. They spent countless hours researching, designing, and testing their system.

The project was ambitious, involving complex algorithms and hardware integration, but Alex was undeterred. He applied everything he had learned over the past years, from technical skills to project management and teamwork.The capstone project was presented at the university's annual engineering showcase. It was a resounding success, earning praise from faculty and industry professionals alike. The project's potential for real-world application attracted attention from several companies, leading to internship offers and collaboration opportunities for Alex and his team.In his final year, Alex also took on a mentoring role, inspired by the support he had received from Dr. Hayes and others. He volunteered as a peer advisor for incoming freshmen, sharing his experiences and offering guidance.He understood the challenges new students faced and was eager to help them navigate their own journeys.One student, Emily, stood out. She reminded Alex of his younger self – ambitious, yet unsure of her path. Alex took her under his wing, helping her with both academic and personal challenges. He introduced her to the innovation club and encouraged her to take part in projects and competitions. Under his mentorship, Emily flourished, gaining confidence and finding her place in the university community.Mentoring Emily and other students was a rewarding experience for Alex. It reinforced his belief in the power of community and support. He realized that his journey was not just about his own success but also about helping others achieve their potential.

As graduation approached, Alex began to reflect more deeply on his future goals. He applied to several graduate programs, focusing on sustainable engineering and technology. His experiences at Northwood and abroad had solidified his desire to work on solutions that could address global challenges such as climate change and resource management.Alex also explored job opportunities, considering positions that would allow him to apply his skills in real-world contexts. He received several offers, including one from a leading tech company interested in his smart grid project. After careful consideration, he decided to accept a research position at a renowned institute dedicated to renewable energy innovations.The role promised to be both challenging and impactful, aligning perfectly with his aspirations.Graduation day was a culmination of Alex's hard work and perseverance. As he walked across the stage to

receive his diploma, he felt a deep sense of accomplishment. His parents were in the audience, beaming with pride.
The journey from a small-town dreamer to a confident, capable graduate had been filled with ups and downs, but each step had been worth it.In his graduation speech, Alex spoke about the importance of resilience, community, and continuous learning. He thanked his mentors, friends, and family for their unwavering support.He encouraged his fellow graduates to pursue their passions and to never give up, no matter the obstacles they might face.With a clear vision for his future, Alex looked forward to the next chapter of his life. He knew that there would be new challenges and opportunities ahead, but he was ready to face them with the same determination and optimism that had carried him through college.As he prepared to step into the world beyond Northwood University, he felt a profound sense of gratitude and excitement for the journey that lay ahead.

Shodiyeva Madina is a teenage girl who has a strong passion to promote peace and empower communites.Till now, she has published more than 10 thought-provoking articles as a way to remind others about the rights we hold as individuals. Madina is a winner of several

national language Olympiads and competitions, one of them being "The best english student of the year". She is enthusiastic about being a polyglot one day.As a thriving youth, she hopes to become a beckon of action and hope for her peers.

I imagine of a sun when justice comes to my mind. The sun doesn't forget a village just because it is small. But, inequality is all around there on earth. The society we live in seems to exaggarate differences of males and females. Take a simple cooking- a skill to nourish oneself as an example. It isn't a secret that this one has mainly been questioned to be whose job. The man who cooks a meal for his family is seen as emasculated or slave to the woman. If the point of gender is about biological differences ,what does it have to do with such daily tasks? The question is: Are women born with cooking genes? Even if it was the case, most of the well-known chefs are known to be males.

People are prone to have separate expectations for women and men. Problem with gender is that it prescribes how we should be rather than recognizing who we are. Stereotypes towards women may go unnoticed in the everyday realm of our lives, but this is actually costing a lot for both sides.

Girls in some countries are under much pressure

from outside regarding the most personal and crucial decisions of life like marriage or career. In most cases, girls are raised to think in a way that the best option is to be a housewife. This restrictive mindset has killed millions of passions before they are even born. I specifically remember having hard time deciding on my career. It was hard not because I had limitless choices but because the options were limited. Admittedly, some are inclined to stay at home and dedicate their life to raising kids. But, there are also those who are enthusiastic about academic and financial development. And, in many communities, the girl who is getting married is forced to give up on a dream, passion or job.

Personally, I think equality is about inclusivity. It is about unique needs and wants of every female. True feminism isn't a concept to define a female but a methodology to accept her way of thinking- to let her believe in her worth and importance in individual decisions. And we, as human beings, should respect that even if we hold up to different beliefs.

I had already been a disappointment for my family before i even came to this world. Why is The birth of a girl waited as unfortunate. People act like they know the trajectory of a girl's whole life and she has less to offer. We have passed the times when some ancient tribes would kill or bury girl babies alive upon being born. But ,we still have a long way in achieving social justice all over the world. According to some entrenched cultural beliefs, you are seen as a resilient woman when you endure violence and still respect your husband. In their way of achieving that social label of an "acceptable women", they are discouraged to reveal about any abuse or threats or pains experienced .But do women have to endure the things that end with the loss of life or health. When i hear about the increasing number of women who are turning to the victims of unhealthy relationships or early marriage, I despise the mindset of people which is letting that cruelty to happen Why does this all happen? From a young age, we teach girls to shrink themselves and make them feel like guilty for being born female. We limit their potential to discover their full potential and be positive change-makers. We forget they are half of this world, half of the population and mothers of future generation.

That mindset of expectations is also detrimental for men. With the thought that they should always stay still and hide their feelings of vulnerability, men mostly suffer mentally because of huge responsibilities. Statistically, it was estimated that men account for a significant of 75 percent of suicide worldwide.

Feminism has been mostly linked to man-hating. But, You don't have to blow out someone's candle to make yours shine brighter. In fact, those countries that are the most gender equal are also countries that stand the highest on the happiness scale. Last question to reflect on: What is the problem in man making dinner for her wife when they are both happy? If only we tried to see things from different angle and helped each other to grow, the world would be a better place. Cultural changes may take a lot of time. But, I believe that everything we do counts such a long way.

Jumaboyeva Navruza is 1st-year student of the Faculty of Romano-Germanic Philology of the Uzbekistan State University of World. She is poet, young translator, activist , leader.

METHODS OF DEVELOPMENT OF ORAL SPEECH IN THE GERMAN LANGUAGE LESSON

State world languages of Uzbekistan

University Romano-Germanic Philology
1st-year student of the faculty
Jumaboeva Navruza

Abstract: Today, the biggest problem of students in teaching the German language is their poor oral speech. Through this article, you will learn how to improve your German speaking skills in a number of ways.

Keywords: speaking skills, oral speech, exercise, speech activity, story, role playing, discussions, brainstorming, interview, news

Speech is the process of creating and exchanging meaning using verbal and non-verbal signs in various contexts. Speaking is an important part of learning and teaching a second language. Despite its importance, the teaching of speaking has been undervalued for many years, and German language teachers have continued to teach speaking skills through methods such as repeating exercises or memorizing dialogues. However, the goal of teaching any language today requires improving students' communicative skills, because only in this way learners can express their thoughts and engage in communication in accordance with social and cultural rules in every communicative situation. Below are some speaking activities that can be used in German classes, along with many methods for speaking teachers and students to teach second language learners to speak effectively.

How can we develop speaking skills?

Many linguists and teachers of German as a second language now point out that students learn to speak a second language through "interaction". Communicative language teaching and cooperative activities are the most effective way to achieve this goal. The formation of speaking skills is based on real life situations. By using this method in German language classes, learners will have the opportunity to communicate with each other in a purposeful way. German language teachers need to create a classroom environment where daily communication, effective activities, and meaningful tasks help students develop their speaking skills. This can occur as a result of students performing tasks in groups to achieve the goal.

Training aimed at speech development , discussions

After a lesson based on a certain topic, teachers can have various discussions with students within the topic. As a result of the discussion, the students set goals and tasks such as coming to an appropriate conclusion within a given issue, exchanging opinions on the topic, or finding a solution to the problem in small groups. Before the discussion, its goals and objectives should be determined by the teacher. Thus, since the discussion process is suitable for this purpose, students do not spend their time talking to each other about trivial things. For example, students can participate in agree/disagree discussions. In this type of discussion, the teacher can form groups of 4 or 5 students each and ask, "Do people learn better when they read or do people learn better when they travel?" can give controversial sentences like Then each group thinks about its topic for a certain period of time and presents its ideas to others.

The important thing is that the winnings should be equally distributed among the members of the group. At the end, the class will determine the winning group that best defended their idea. This activity develops critical thinking and quick decision-making, and students learn to express themselves politely and defend their opinions, even if they do not agree with the opinions of other groups. For effective group discussions, it is recommended not to form large groups, as students who cannot quickly engage in discussions may avoid participating in large groups. Group members are assigned by the teacher or students themselves, but in each discussion activity the groups should be rearranged so that students can work with different people and receive different ideas. Finally, regardless of the purpose of class or group discussions, students should always be encouraged to ask questions, express opinions, and support them.

Role play

Another way to encourage students to speak German is through role playing. Learners imagine themselves in different social situations and in different social roles. In role plays, the teacher gives the students information such as who they are, what they think or feel. For example, the teacher can say to the student "You are Anna, you will go to the doctor and tell what happened yesterday and...".

Fill in the information

In this activity, students should work in pairs. One learner will have information that their partner does not have, and partners will share their information. Information space activities serve many purposes, such as problem solving or information gathering. In addition, each participant plays an important role, because the task cannot be completed if the partners do not provide the necessary information to others. These activities are effective because everyone has the opportunity to speak at length in the language they are learning.

The story

Learners can summarize a fable or story they have heard before or create their own story to tell their classmates. The story develops creative thinking. It also teaches students how to start, develop, and end an idea, including how to express characters and the process of a story. Students can tell riddles or jokes. For example, at the beginning of each lesson, the teacher can call several students and give short riddles or jokes. Thus, the teacher not only appeals to the speaking ability of the students, but also attracts the attention of the class.

Interviews

Students can conduct conversations with different people on selected topics. The teacher gives the students instructions about the types of questions they can ask or the order of the process, but the students must prepare the interview questions themselves. Conversations with people give students the opportunity to practice speaking skills not only in class, but also outside the class process and help them socialize. After the interview, each student must present his work to the class. In addition, students can interview each other and "introduce" their partner to the class.

Completing the story

This is a fun, whole-audience speaking activity with students sitting in a circle. For this activity, the teacher starts telling a story, but after a few sentences, he stops telling the story. Then each student begins to tell the story from where the previous one left off. Each student should add four to ten sentences. Students can add new characters, events, descriptions, etc.

News
Before coming to class, students are asked to read a newspaper or magazine and tell their friends about the most interesting news they found. They can tell their friends about something worth telling about in their daily life.

Describe the picture
Another way to use pictures in speaking activities is to give students one picture and have them describe what is in the picture. For this activity, groups are formed and each group is given a different picture. Students discuss the picture with their groups, and then a representative from each group describes the picture to the whole class. This activity develops students' creativity and imagination, as well as public speaking skills.

Find the difference
For this activity, students work in pairs and each pair is given two different pictures, for example a picture of boys playing football and another picture of girls playing tennis. In pairs, students discuss the similarities and differences between the pictures.

Conclusion
Developing speaking skills is a very important part of learning a foreign language (German). The ability to communicate clearly and effectively in a foreign language contributes to a student's success in school and later in every stage of life. That is why I think that language teachers should pay

great attention to improving speech. It is necessary to provide a rich environment in which meaningful communication takes place, rather than encouraging language learners only to memorize. To this end, the various speaking activities listed above greatly contribute to the development of students' basic interactive skills necessary for life. I think that these activities will increase students' activity in the learning process and at the same time make the learning process meaningful and interesting for them

LIST OF REFERENCES
1. Chaney, A.L. and T.L. Burke. 1998. Teaching Oral Communication in Grades K-8. Boston: Allyn & Bacon
2. Selce-Murcia. M. 2001. Teaching English as a Second or Foreign Language (Phase 3). USA: Heinle & Heinle.
3. Brown, G. and G. Yule. 1983. Teaching Oral Language. Cambridge: Cambridge University Press.
4. "Modern methods in foreign language teaching methodology" Zayniddin Sanakulov

Her full name is Hatamova Charos Shavkatjon qizi. Born in 2009 in Fergana region. Currently, she is studying at the creative school named after Erkin Vahidov organized by PIIMA. Her creative works have been published in several international magazines. The artist's future goal is to become a poetess, to receive the Zulfiya state award and to become a scholar of literature.

Over my pains
chimneys,
A terrible horror is coming.
It touches my heart
black and white world
It breaks my heart
blood colored figure.

Slowly, slowly
whispering
I will tell you my pains
to magicians.
Tonight, this morning before my eyes,
I told you about my problems
to papers.

My heart is calm, good morning
enough
He smiles slowly
the moon is shining.
My dreams lead to mornings
but,
Ottomans fly blue
in the blanket.

The memory of the black hawks
To destroy anyway
I can't stand it.
Not enough wings, high

to the flight
Even a hawk does not swallow a "friend" who calls.

"Kimlar" burned in the grass from pain
coming up
A few screams were heard.
Hearts burned in the grass are painful
Aritar
I found words worlds.

Her full name, Avazbekova Mubinabonu Dilshodbek qizi, was born on May 29, 2005 in Korgontepa district of Andijan region. Currently, she is a student of the 2nd stage of the National University of Uzbekistan named after Mirzo Ulugbek. Winner of many Olympiads and participant of successful projects.

The effective methods of teaching foreign languages in secondary education institutions.

Avazbekova Mubina Dilshodbek qizi,
Mirzo Ulug'bek named Uzbekistan National University,
Faculty of Foreign Philology, Department of Philology and Teaching Languages, 2nd year student (+998930070104)
@bonuavazovaavazovagmail.com

Annotation: The article presents observations on effective methods of teaching foreign languages in secondary education institutions. The importance of learning foreign languages is significant both in Uzbekistan and in other countries. The most effective methods of teaching foreign languages are presented in the article. In addition to this, the annotation highlights the organization of lessons in an interesting manner and the creation of intensive classes using computer programs during the process of teaching foreign languages, as well as the use of audio and colorful materials.

Main Section: Important Methods in Teaching Foreign Languages Individual and Interactive Lessons: Working with students individually in the process of teaching foreign languages acquires significant importance. The intended goal is to enhance the speaking and listening skills of children learning foreign languages. Creating an engaging classroom atmosphere is more important than any teaching method. It can be challenging to manage the ability of children to control themselves and maintain their attention throughout the entire lesson.

Indeed, therefore, it is necessary for educators to present songs, poems, or animated cartoons that children enjoy listening to in order to improve their listening skills.

Using audio-visual aids: In secondary education institutions, using various colorful and visual video materials while teaching foreign languages increases students' interest in these languages. Nowadays, all modern classrooms are equipped with multimedia devices. Children are being taught English not only through songs but also through poems and stories, as well as video clips. Utilizing multimedia provides great opportunities for teachers to teach. Through this method, we can further enhance children's language skills. For instance, if our topic is "Fruits," before teaching the names of various fruits, we can use their sounds, which captures the attention of children. Starting with these interesting sounds like "banana, apple, orange..." makes learning fruit names more engaging.

Active games and engaging children: Instead of simply conducting foreign language classes, if we incorporate games, the interest of young children in foreign languages will increase even more. Moreover, their level of activity will also increase. For example, organizing games in the form of relay races among children. In this, children are divided into two groups, and they need to form words from hidden letters, and the winning team receives rewards. Competitions among children are very important because they help develop a sense of competition from a young age. As a result, each child becomes more interested in foreign languages.

Textbooks and Teaching Materials: Textbooks and teaching materials for learning foreign languages can be very useful. Websites and online learning resources, such as Duolingo, BBC Languages, open up many opportunities for learning various foreign languages. These websites make learning interactive and provide learners with the opportunity to learn at their own pace. Platforms like Kids English offer many foreign language learning courses. These courses make it convenient for learners to study the languages they are interested in. Indeed, YouTube and TED Talks provide opportunities to find and understand discussions and texts in many languages. You Tube and TED Talks provide the opportunity to find and understand discussions and texts in many languages. This is beneficial for making learning easy and interesting. Pedagogical skills play a crucial role in teaching language, ensuring successful learning outcomes, increasing motivation, and making the learning process convenient and effective. Debates and practical exercises incorporated into lessons: Engaging students in debates and practical exercises is a useful method in language learning. It helps them to develop skills in listening, expressing ideas, and using language in conversations, thus enhancing their language proficiency.

Lessons conducted in a question-answer format: Lessons incorporating debates and practical exercises: Engaging students in discussions and practical activities is a beneficial method in language learning. This approach helps them to improve their skills in listening, expressing ideas, and strengthening their vocabulary and language usage through conversation practice.

Verdict: The aim outlined in the article is to find solutions to the challenges faced in teaching foreign languages effectively in today's educational institutions. Practical activities, interactive lessons, and audio-visual aids have gained significant importance in teaching foreign languages in schools. Children's learning of foreign languages is considered crucial for their future.

Key words: interactive, audio-visual, individual, intensive, multimedia Platform: Duolingo

List of utilized literature:
David A. J, Eggen, P Kauchak. Methods for Teaching: Promoting student learning [M] 2002.
https://www.linkedin.com
https://www.innosci.org
https://www.researchgate.net

THE CONCEPT OF CRIMINAL ATTEMPTS IN CRIMINAL LAW

Sobirjonova Sevinch Akmaljon qizi
Email: sevinchsobirjanova05@gmail.com
The student of Namangan State University, faculty of law (jurisprudence by type of activity)

Annotation: The second stage of unfinished criminal activity is attempted crime. Attempt is defined as intentional actions (inaction) of a person directly aimed at committing a crime, if the crime was not completed due to circumstances beyond the control of this person. An attempt constitutes an action directly aimed at achieving a criminal result. Immediacy means that the offender has begun to carry out an act that forms the objective side of the crime. This is what makes an assassination attempt different from the first stage preparation. Thus, the preparation of a passport or civilian clothing by a military personnel for the purpose of evading military service constitutes preparation for desertion. This article reveals the concept and types of attempted crimes.

Keywords: Intentional attempts, an incomplete crime, concept of criminal attempts, attempted burglary, direct action, criminal code.

The concept of attempt refers to an incomplete or inchoate crime where an individual initially was intended to commit a crime and undertook specific actions to complete it but ultimately failed to commit a full offense due to some accidental causes. The legal definition of criminal attempt in which the defendant ultimately fails to pull off the crime varies from state to state. Generally, charges for attempt are filed when an individual has the actual intent to commit a crime and takes direct action toward completing the crime but fails. Once a crime is actually completed, you can no longer be charged with criminal attempt. You cannot be convicted of both criminal attempt and the crime itself. For example, imagine that you drive to a stranger's house with a bag of lockpicking tools. Your goal is to break in and steal the homeowner's cash, electronics, and other belongings. Unfortunately (or fortunately), your lockpicking skills aren't what they used to be, and you can't get into the dwelling. If law enforcement shows up just as you are attempting, for the third time, to pick the lock, you can be charged with attempted burglary. You cannot be charged with an actual burglary because you were not successful in gaining entry to the stranger's home. Certain elements of crime, the so-called truncated ones, are such in their design that they are considered completed both when harmful consequences occur and when actions are committed. The commission of an act that does not entail socially dangerous consequences, in relation to these offenses, does not constitute an attempt, but a completed crime. So, I., intending to kill a police officer, attacked him with a knife, but the victim managed to disarm the attacker. I.'s actions were qualified as a completed crime - an attempt on the life of a law enforcement officer. An attempt to commit one crime (as well as preparation) can form a complete corpus delicti of another crime. Such attacks contain two crimes and must be classified as a whole. For example, an attacker, trying to break into a store, breaks a window and is detained at the crime scene. Such actions are qualified by a combination of crimes: attempted theft. Depending on the degree of completion of the actions intended by the perpetrator, attempts are divided into two types: completed and unfinished. The attempt is considered completed if the perpetrator has performed all the actions that, in his opinion, are sufficient to achieve the criminal result, but the latter did not occur due to circumstances beyond his control. For example, a killer pulls the trigger of a pistol, but it misfires, or a shot is fired, but the mortally wounded victim is cured thanks to prompt medical care; a thief takes a box out of the room where, according to his calculations, there should be valuables, but in reality there were none there. The Criminal Code of the Republic of Uzbekistan, adopted on 22 September 1994 and comed into force on 1 April 1995, it is the only source of criminal law. It should be noted, that the criminality, penality and other legal consequences of the criminal act are determined only by the Criminal Code of the Republic of Uzbekistan. The aim of the Criminal Code is to protect the individual, his rights and freedoms, interests of society and the state from criminal encroachments. A person who commits a crime, in order to achieve the result of a criminal commits certain acts and wants to attack criminal consequences. But, in some cases as a result of these acts a person does not achieve his pursued aim. Although in such cases there is no encroachment on the specific social relations, it is not harmful, but there is a public danger.

Therefore, the criminal law establishes criminal liability for an uncompleted crime - preparation for crime and criminal attempt. The word „attempt", said chief justice Cockburn, clearly conveys with it the idea that if the attempt had succeeded, the offence charged would have been committed. In other words, attempt is the direct movement towards the commission of an offence after the preparation has been made. According to English law, a person may be guilty of an attempt to commit an offence, if he does an act which is more than merely preparatory to the commission of the offence and a person may be guilty or attempt to commit an offence even though the facts are such that the commission the offence is impossible2. In accordance with Article 14 of the Criminal Code of the Republic of Uzbekistan, A culpable socially dangerous act (action or inaction) prohibited by this Code on pain of imposing of a penalty shall be recognized as a crime. So, according to this definition, any action or inaction shall be recognized as a crime only in the presence of public danger, illegality, guilt, penality. This rule applies in relation to uncompleted crime. Criminal Attempt is socially dangerous (causes or a real threat of damage to social relations, protected by the Criminal Code), illegal (prohibited by the Criminal Code), punishable (shall be punished in accordance with articles 54, 58 of the Criminal

Code), guilty (conscious volitional activity entity) act. Attempt is the direct movement towards the commission of an offence after the preparation is made3. Attempt - an action (inaction) directly aimed at the commission of an offence, which is not brought to an end due to circumstances not depending of a committer, or onset of action (or inaction) directly aimed at the commission of an offence and contains a specific objective evidence of a crime. Attempt is the second stage of the commission of the offense, a conscious action, reflecting the objective side of an offence to commit a crime and the attainment of socially dangerous consequences, which finished due to circumstances not depending of a committer. Attempt is the second stage of the crime characterized by the beginning of the crime. At the stage of committing a criminal attempt is carried out part of the objective side of a particular crime, it is the action or inaction referred in the disposition of the article of the Special Part of Criminal Code is carried out in full or in part, however, the criminal result is not achieved. Under the criminal result should be understood not only the consequences of criminal offenses with the material composition, but also uncompleted perform actions or inactions referred to the crimes with the formal composition.

Summarizing what has been said, we can

highlight the following signs of attempted crime:
1) the beginning of the commission of a crime;
2) forced interruption (objective sign);
3) the presence of direct intent (subjective sign).

In the theory of criminal law, the point of view has been proven, according to which attempted crime can take place both in material and formal compositions. The fact that if a crime is committed with indirect intent a person foresees the possibility occurrence of socially dangerous consequences in as a result of its actions does not mean that it tries to achieve their implementation. On the contrary, when the person does not desire this form of guilt, but only allows it the occurrence of these consequences. It is for this reason that an attempted crime with indirect intent is impossible.

References:
1. The Constitution of the Republic of Uzbekistan (amended March 2016)
2. The Criminal Code of the Republic of Uzbekistan (amended March 2016)
3. Rustambayev M.X. The Republic of Uzbekistan Criminal Law course. –Tashkent. Ilm Ziyo. 2010, P.246.
4. Usmonaliyev M. The composition of offense (corpus delicti). -Tashkent: TSIL, 2008. -P.8.
5. Turgunboyev E.O. The foundation of qualifing

act as a criminal attempt // The bulletin of Supreme Court of the Republic of Uzbekistan. 2008, №5. –P.35.

6.Rajib Hassan The Elements and Stages of a Crime An Overview.

7.The Resolution of the Supreme Court Plenum of the Republic of Uzbekistan (24.09.2004) "About judicial practice of intentional killing" №13.

8.Kozlov A.P. The doctrine on stages of crime. – Saint Petersburg. -P. 289.

9.Nazarenko A.G., Sitnikova A.I. Unfinished crimes and its types: Monograph. -M.: OS-89, 2003. -P. 108. 12. Anisimov A.A. Unfinished crimes and the proving specifics. 10.Dissertation. 2003. -P.51-52. 13. Criminal Law. Textbook. – Tashkent: The Academy of MIA of the Republic of Uzbekistan, 2012. -P. 225. 14. The Digest of Law of the Republic of Uzbekistan, 2008 y., №16, Article 116

11.https://sdo.academy-skrf.ru/extbook/up_obch/public_html/page67.html

12.https://www.researchgate.net/publication/344457979_ATTEMPT_IN_CRIMINAL_LAW_OF_THE_REPUBLIC_OF_UZBEKISTAN

13.https://en.wikipedia.org/wiki/Criminal_Attempts_Act_1981

14.https://lawexplores.com/criminal-attempts/

Global governance in the 21st century: international order and the need to reconstruct international institutions.

Author
Yusufjonov Bahrom,
scientific researcher, 1st year student of the Uzbekistan State University of world languages, international relations

Annotation : As we all know, political crises in the international arena, a weakening of trust between states in international politics, a decrease in the legitimacy of institutions with a global position threaten the stable riviocalization of humanity. In order to find solutions to these problems, it is necessary to initially modernize universal organizations and organize their activities in a monand way to the specific economic and political environment of the developing 21st century. This article will talk about the origin of the dilemmas mentioned above, the appearance of the international order today, the place of international organizations in the solution of current issues and alternative options aimed at their solution.

Keywords: international institutions, International Governance Order, international community, veto power, legitimacy , representative system serious issues of the present era, accelerated globalization of the world, non-fulfillment of the terms of the treaty aimed at limiting mass and nuclear weapons, environmental crises, immigration problems, disintegration of states in the international arena, the origin of ideological and religious conflicts, the growing distrust of international law and organizations and similar pressing problems are causing unrest in the international arena, the weakening of collective cooperation and their departure from human control (Kissenger world order) [1]. On top of that, international institutions that are actually supposed to regulate international activities, cooperation, and receive socio-political, economic and environmental threats are making the situation worse as a result of its dysfunctional activities. In order to find solutions to these problems and alleviate the situation, the world community must carry out its collective and rapid actions in modernizing the foundations of international governance, international order and the activities of international institutions. In this regard, it is advisable to start reforms in terms of coverage from the domestic activities of international universal organizations: UN, (United Nations), its UNSC (Security Council), WB (World Bank), IMF (International Monetary Fund), G8 (Big Eight: USA, Canada, Western Europe and Japan). Because these organizations have a significant role in the international arena, both in terms of coverage and in terms of impact. It is also possible to form a multipolar world order based on equal opportunities and powers by developing a system of representation in organizations and the distribution of powers.

What is international order itself?

According to the Princeton University Encyclopedia (Encyclopedia Princetoniensis, author: Richard Falk) World Order as a term is sometimes used as an analytical, and sometimes as a guideline. Both applications serve important purposes in understanding the realities of political life on a global scale. From an analytical point of view, world order refers to the regulation of power and authority that provides the basis for behavior. The meaning of diplomacy and world politics on a Global scale. According to the guidelines, world order refers to the preferred order of power and authority associated with the realization of values such as peace, economic growth and equality, human rights, environmental quality and sustainability.[2]

In addition, we can say that in the formation of international order, the activities of international institutions, their legitimacy are of great importance, as well as the effectiveness of activities, issues of cooperation in the international arena, political and economic trends. In general the term originated in the context of explaining the political situation that arose after the first and second world wars, political institutions and the mechanism of international politics that arose as a result of them. Later, the world political scene became a branch of the bipolar order (the dependence of the United States and the USSR) and the unipolar order (the transformation of the United States into a single global force in the period from the breakup of the USSR to the formation of new centers of power) during the Cold War. And now the term multipolar world order is used a lot, but at the moment the world order is very complex in structure. According to us lik political scientist Ian Bremmer, there are 3 Different World orders in the world in the current period . These are international security, economic and digital information procedures [3]. In the field of international security, the US-led Euroatlantic bloc (NATO) continues to be the leading force . The functioning of this system, on the other hand, leads to a number of problems, and the main of them are geopolitical conflicts between the collective West and Russia. It is these contradictions that the two-way standards are being formed in tufuayli international politics, and the struggle between the two powers, as opposed to the norms of international law in particular the treaties on weapons of mass destruction (on the limitation of strategic weapons), is losing its legitimacy. Looking at the economic environment, we will be able to see the abundance of relatively leading actors here . For example, the United States,China, Japan, the European Union are the largest economic players, and more than 10 countries can be added to their list, including India, Pakistan, Brazil again. But in this regard, we must mention that in the near term, China's economic growth in very large pictures, the Chinese economy reaching the US economy and passing it on some fronts, and the fact that these economic achievements are also Joe to Chinese foreign policy, has resulted in a change in the US's view of China. And now the United States sees China as its biggest potential rival, rather than Russia, and uses several ways to influence it, including the Taiwan issue. The third category of international order is today's actual issue . Today, the role of the no doubt digital information industry in providing information to people, societies, forming their views, thoughts is great in benihoya . Because the fact that we live in a post-industrial society, the need for information in the economy, politics, science, social life, increases us in our dependence on large social networks, corporatisses, which are the main drivers of today's information.' As a result, however, states ' enthusiasm for managing the information Sox is growing significantly, with zeroki controlling the world that controls information. The collision of some negative in these 3 procedures remains the main causes of problems in the modern system of international relations .

What does the concept of international organizations (institutions) mean ?

INTERNATIONAL ORGANIZATIONS. The National Society (Association), which is not under the care of states or government, is an IARI Association formed to achieve common goals in political, economic, social, science and technology, culture and the like; one of the most important forms of multilateral cooperation between states. International organizations arose in the XIX century, and after the Second World War many began to be formed. Currently, the number of international organizations is more than 4 thousand boiib, and 300 of ulaming are intergovernmental organizations. International organizations are distinguished by a number of specific features. In particular, the structure of international organization will be a constituent document (charter), which sets the main goal and directions of the organization's activities; such organizations will operate continuously or periodically; multilateral negotiations and discussion of problems are the main method of their activities; decisions will be made by vote or consensus; decisions, as a rule, will have the power of recommendation. Intergovernmental international organizations and international non-governmental organizations are distinguished, as well as universal and regional organizations. Mas., ILO, MAG ATE, UN International Court of justice, UN High Commissioner for refugee affairs, World Health Organization, World Intellectual Property Organization, and b. International organizations are called Organization, Union, Savings, bank, agency, Center and so on. 0 ' The Republic of Uzbekistan is an equal member of more than 50 prestigious international organizations. These are the Central Asian Cooperation Organization, The Tashkent treaty (ODKB), TurkSoy, the Union of Turkic states and b [4]. It can be seen that the scope of the goals and objectives of international organizations is much wider, and in a sense, their role in the overall sustainable development is greater.

Figure I-2 DIRECTION OF THE WORLD
Percent saying "wrong direction"

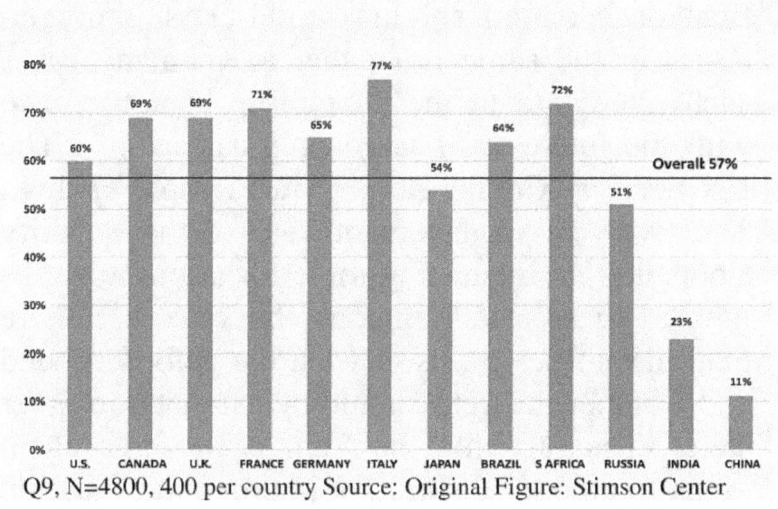

Q9, N=4800, 400 per country Source: Original Figure: Stimson Center

Most of the people (57%) represented by the countries G7 and BRICS say that there is no information about the world on the road, which is evidenced by the widespread stonework on World Affairs (see figure i-2). Only 30% say they are moving around the world by road. . In terms of negative views, 10 of the 12 states again dominate the population. Most games are in Italy (77% wrong way), South Africa (72%), France (71%). Many are people with similar views in North America (US 60%, Canada 69%) and other European countries [6]. Of course, the importance of these thoughts was given by the Foreign situation and the importance of this tension of the global Tashkent khissasi Kham. Also international organizations do not have a final decision on solving world-class important issues at the same time, that is, in many cases such issues are in the next place in accordance with the interests of large political actors . The UN Security Council is a vivid example of this . The five-year management veto of the Security Council is an interesting topic for a long time, as long as these states embody the veto. It is here that questions arise as to what the veto is needed and whether the veto should be extended to other states. The fact that the Veto power was again given to other states did not improve the situation . When a representative from each region is given a veto, Ham, who does not guarantee the protection of the interests of each representative is Hech . Here it was advisable to consider information and issues about the prestige of the General Assembly on the basis of the work and equal rights of each representative here. To date, five years of education at a time when the world is face-to-face with great challenges to solve the fate of the world injustice and Rejeb Tayyip Erdogan said that the world in fair and sustainable development is shaking the answers for all states [7] .While common occurs in the UN (United Nations) and UNDP (Security Council), minorities today have also been seen in other international organizations such as the World Bank, IMF (International Monetary Fund), WTO (World Trade Organization). In international organizations, all azo representatives are obliged to have the same powers and opportunities in solving issues within this Tashkent and which Tashkent aims to find a solution for itself. But as you can see above, there are major shortcomings in the activities of international organizations, in the game of states with a large definition of the main role in Tashkent, there will be no opportunity to protect their rights and opportunities in local small states. Another aspect of the problem is that global institutions have nothing to do with serious problems. Not international problems, but big games are the interests of people primarily in appearance. Because of this, the upheavals of human rights are turning a blind eye to environmental integrity and actions that threaten the future of humanity. These processes mean that the international community needs to do its job to ensure a desired, peaceful future .

The international management industry should cover a number of goals and objectives. First of all, it is necessary to give equal rights and opportunities to each representative of political institutions. That is, the resolution of issues should only be given to small states other than giving them to large ones, so that ham can protect their interests. As such, it is possible to ensure that nations that are politically composed do not have international governance stuck abroad and that their interests are not undermined . The main aspect of the reforms should be the wide scope and collectivism of this international institution . Currently, current issues are relevant to the entire international community, and not to the information or territory in terms of coverage. In the latest work of these issues, each member of the global Institute needs to see his own activist, the institutions of public education in Kham, their activist for the borders of the state . That is, the movement of the foundations of international law of cooperation at the international level should be strong. The United Nations and the United Nations also look at the performance of their activities in a qualitative way to improve the effectiveness of large Tashkent and ensure the coercion of the decisions they make to address the places where they take place today . Because even today, the resolutions or resolutions developed by the UN do not have enough fundamental power in solving pressing issues, in understanding their effectiveness and, in turn, in bringing them to the highest parable of these issues. Of course international organizations, management order organizations are very large topics and need a time interval of information to increase them in practice . But if the mentioned aspects are paid attention to and cooperation is established in the collective for the implementation of these projects, it will be much easier to achieve the goals seen .

List of literature used:
1. World order, Henry Kissinger
2. Princeton Encyclopedia of self-determination, Richard Falk
3. TEDxTalks ted.com/watch/tedx-talks
4. Isokhli Dictionary of diplomatic terms, Israel Shamsimukhammedov
5. https://www.brookings.edu/articles/reform-of-global-governance-priorities-for-action/
6. May be fair around the world, Rajap Tayyip Erdoğan
7. Global governance survey 2023, STIMSON

www.ingramcontent.com/pod-product-compliance
Lightning Source LLC
LaVergne TN
LVHW010610070526
838199LV00063BA/5128